I0214687

LETTERS TO GOD

TRANSFORMING CRISIS INTO CONSCIOUSNESS

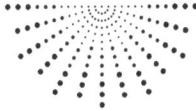

PATRICIA A. LYNCH, BSCHE, MBA

MINGUS MOUNTAIN PUBLISHERS LLC

Copyright © 2018 by Patricia A. Lynch

All rights reserved.

No part of this book may be reproduced in any form or by any electronic or mechanical means, including information storage and retrieval systems, without written permission from the author, except for the use of brief quotations in a book review.

Tradepaper ISBN-13: 978-1-948483-00-1

eBook ISBN-13: 978-1-948483-01-8

Library of Congress Control Number: 2018908781

Published by Mingus Mountain Publishers LLC, Cottonwood, Arizona

Cover design by Daniel Valencia.

CONTENTS

INTRODUCTION

Be careful what you ask for! My mother was fond of that expression. I have heard my spiritual teacher, the late Dr. David Hawkins, use it, too. Maybe I didn't fully realize what might be delivered when I asked God for assistance in letting go of the mind's attachments and aversions.

But God gave me exactly what I asked for and delivered a personalized, ego-busting consciousness crash course. No New Age angelic music, no rainbows, no hearts, no flowers, no butterflies. Just a harrowing ride on the biggest rollercoaster at the amusement park. All dips, turns, flips, drop-offs, and stomach-churning g-forces.

My rollercoaster, the crisis that birthed this book, was a serious flare-up of autoimmune disease that turned life upside-down and presented a challenge to the ego that brought its wily ways to the surface to be processed.

During a time-out of many months on the sofa, body and brain function slowed to the point where everything was experienced through the haze of suspended animation. The low physical energy and the removal of life's ordinary rhythms and distractions, which the ego wanted to interpret as a crisis on the physical plane, created a perfect opportunity to fulfill the intention to evolve consciousness on the spiritual plane.

Wave after wave of willfulness disguised as attractions, aversions, opinions, judgments, and resistances rolled in like the surf crashing on a beach. It was all about willfulness to control outcome. There was the attraction to being well and the aversion to being ill, wanting life to go according to plan and schedule, opinions of the ego, judgment of self and others, and endless resistances that seemed absurd when the rising tide threatened extinction of the body.

As the crisis deepened, I set the intention and took actions to heal the physical body, which I honor as the vehicle for the divine soul, but I continually practiced releasing any attachment to outcome.

I chatted with God along the way, continually affirming spiritual tenets and asking for the gifts of strength, discernment, and acceptance. I also expressed gratitude, even on the darkest days.

I eventually converted my early morning practice from mental prayer to handwritten missives when I realized handwriting practice could help me recover fine motor skills that had been damaged by brain inflammation. When I began writing letters to God, physical improvement was rapid, but the greatest benefit was spiritual.

The combined effect of putting pen to paper (engaging parts of the brain that process the senses of sight and touch) and writing about the positive topics of intention, gratitude, and supplication had a synergistic effect. Compared to silent, mental communication, the handwritten missives imprinted everything more deeply in the brain and the soul. The morning ritual of writing a letter to God also predisposed me to view the spiritual and life lessons available in every moment throughout the day, not just during the challenge of crisis.

Many days, the available energy level limited the letter to one or two challenges or to the reaffirmations of spiritual beliefs such as *all is in divine order*. Other days, I wrote longer letters to God when I had more energy or more to process. As the letters accumulated, I began to reread them for a spiritual boost.

When I shared some letters with friends who

have widely differing spiritual philosophies, they all found something to ponder or something that made them think differently about ordinary life situations. That sparked the idea for this memoir, each chapter of which is a letter to God accompanied by brief commentary to provide context.

The content is deceptively simple, but it meets the reader at whatever depth is appropriate. The book may be read from cover to cover, or chapters may be selected randomly or by topic. The letters are good companions for contemplation, because they cover basic spiritual philosophies that apply to daily life.

Some days, I am drawn to read and contemplate specific subjects such as *Choosing Happiness*, *Letting Go of the Judge*, *Surrendering Impatience*, or *Releasing Attachment to Outcome*. Other days, I need the humor of *Microsoft as Spiritual Teacher!* or the light-hearted *Expressing Gratitude* or *Witnessing Beauty*.

Regardless of how you use this book, if these letters inspire or uplift you, the lessons I learned through illness will have served a divine purpose I never imagined when this journey began.

1. LETTING GO OF WILLFULNESS

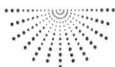

Dear Lord:

Thank you for improving my discernment, for
allowing the knowingness to emerge that
there is no doer.

It is my intention to serve the highest good
this day.

That which serves the highest good will flow
through me effortlessly when the time
is right.

I am merely an instrument, and the personal
ego and opinion block discernment of the
highest good.

It is my intention to use the intellectual gifts I
have been granted to serve the highest
good as that purpose emerges.

Gloria in Excelsis Deo!

I have heard the spiritual teaching that willfulness is of the ego, that it is the source of the belief that there is an individual doer of actions. I have heard that great spiritual progress is made when one lets go of willfulness, the ego's opinion of how things should be, and embraces willingness, the Self accepting the divine perfection of what things are.

I practiced letting go of willfulness, and I thought I was making pretty good progress. But then autoimmune disease smacked me down, robbed the body of energy and forced many months of inactivity.

The choice was mine: I could view illness as either a spiritual teacher or an excuse to fall into victimhood. I chose the former, but it was obvious that it is much easier to talk the talk than walk the walk on the spiritual path!

My former careers in the business world gave me ample opportunities to practice willfulness, and old habits die hard. My actions are not always in alignment with my intentions, but when I let go of willfulness, events flow effortlessly.

2. LETTING GO OF OPINIONS

DEAR LORD:

Today I hope to remember that the opinions
others have of me are none of my business,
that their opinions represent the
projections of their egos, and that my
opinion of their opinions is a projection of
my ego.

I ask for the strength to live this day in
alignment with the intention to receive
and to give the gifts of loving kindness and
undivided attention without judgment or
opinion.

Living life in alignment with these principles
is living life as a prayer.

GLORIA IN EXCELSIS DEO!

I have heard that all opinions are projections of the ego and are therefore not personal. The onset of serious illness evoked strong opinions in myself and others about everything from dietary choices to treatment options.

Early on, when others criticized the choices I made, the ego responded defensively. Contemplation revealed that the defensiveness reflected my own uncertainties. Realizing that the attempts of others to control my journey were projections of their own fears of death (mine and/or theirs) helped me let go of my opinion of their behavior. It was their problem, and it had nothing to do with me.

Letting go of opinions others had about the course of the illness—why I had it, how I could get rid of it, what I should do about it—also opened the door for me to let go of their opinions about *me*. I didn't need to do anything to try to win favor with anyone.

The inner knowingness came that it was right to forge my own path, independent of the opinions of friends, family members, or healthcare providers. It also offered the opportunity to set appropriate boundaries without guilt, to cut the cords of entanglement with others, and to limit contact with controlling people or let them go completely.

3. EXPRESSING GRATITUDE

GOOD MORNING, LORD!

It is another day during which I choose
    happiness and joy and to see the divine in
    all things.

I am grateful for all spiritual teachings that are
    true, and I release all attractions, aversions
    and opinions that block discernment and
    knowingness.

GLORIA IN EXCELSIS DEO!

I have been taught that gratitude and
    happiness are choices that are always
available regardless of external circumstances.

But it wasn't always easy to be grateful, and it was

impossible to be happy when living in a state of resistance. I had to let go resisting the experience of illness, let go the willfulness to be healthy.

While I practiced letting go resisting, I found that an attitude of gratitude helped weaken the ego's resistance to all things it didn't like. Under trying circumstances, it was easier for the ego to allow gratitude than happiness, and gratitude cracked open the door to happiness.

4. CANCELING NEGATIVE BELIEF SYSTEMS

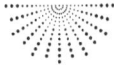

Dear Lord:

I cancel all negative belief systems, including those that pertain to the health and maintenance of the body.

I am grateful to all the cells of the body that function in perfect coordination with one another to support health.

The body absorbs beneficial energy frequencies from the field and is exempt from all negative energy or opinions.

The microbiome flourishes to support perfect functioning of the gut and the brain. The adrenal glands are strong, and the body is synchronized to optimal circadian rhythms.

The communications between brain and body,

as well as body and brain, are in perfect accordance with divine will.

I pray for guidance regarding stewardship of my mental, emotional, physical, and financial gifts.

I dedicate this day to serving the highest good, and I ask the Holy Spirit for guidance, today and always.

I am thankful for the love, kindness, and support of family, friends, neighbors, and perfect strangers.

I intend to be kind, unconditionally loving, and compassionate to all living beings without exception, beginning with myself.

GLORIA IN EXCELSIS DEO!

I have heard the spiritual teaching that canceling negative belief systems that reside in the conscious and subconscious mind is a necessary component of recovery from illness, because what we hold in mind tends to manifest in the body. The placebo effect in medicine is an example of the positive aspects of this principle.

I remind myself to constantly cancel negative belief systems as I hear them and to bring unchallenged negative belief systems to the surface to be canceled. When I hear a television commercial suggesting I have some newly-invented malady that requires pharmaceutical treatment, I emphatically cancel the belief system and avow that I am exempt from it. When a medical professional states that autoimmune disease can never be cured, only put in remission, I silently and firmly cancel that belief system, too.

I hold positive thoughts in mind for the cells and organs of the body, and I express appreciation for them and affirm their perfection.

5. EMBRACING SPIRITUAL LESSONS

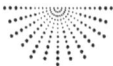

DEAR LORD:

Today I am grateful for all the gifts I have
been given, and I pray for the strength to
always discern the essence and beauty of
each life lesson in events and
circumstances that the world and my
personal ego deem negative or tragic.

I comfort myself in the belief that all is in
divine order at all times, regardless of
external circumstances or the condition of
the physical body.

I remind myself that I have a body, but I am
not a body. I am eternal Spirit.

I am thankful for all the love and support
present in this life, for the blessings of
healing foods, for the beauty of nature

outside my window, and for all the basics
that support life.

I ask for guidance to serve the highest good,
and I ask for the biochemistry that
supports my intention to be patient and
kind to all, including myself.

GLORIA IN EXCELSIS DEO!

J believe in the eternal soul. How can death of the body, which is merely the vehicle for the soul, be bad? The human condition itself is mortal. What difference does it make if I leave this world now or twenty years from now? Either way, the span of this physical lifetime is less than a speck of dust in the eons of eternity.

Illness is an advanced course in spirituality, but enrollment is optional. Illness has helped me fulfill spiritual intention, teaching deep lessons when I open the heart and the doorway to the soul. The intellect on which I relied for decades in the business world is of no use here.

Illness continues to facilitate the transformation of spiritual teachings from intellectual belief to experiential reality. An abrupt exit would have robbed me of these opportunities!

6. CHOOSING HAPPINESS

DEAR LORD:

I am grateful for this day, and I set the intention to be happy and kind no matter what happens.

I pray for divine guidance to serve the highest good at each moment and to relinquish my opinions, which are all based on the ego and the intellect and therefore mean nothing.

I pray for the relief of suffering of all sentient beings, including myself.

I hold in mind all who are lonely, afraid, depressed, discouraged, or ill. May divine light shine upon them all to give them solace and comfort.

I am grateful for all the gifts I have in life:

what is left of my health, material
comforts, and loving friends and family.
I ask for discernment to guide me on how I
can best use these gifts, including the
intellect, for the benefit of mankind.
I accept completely whatever level of health
and vigor supports the stewardship of my
assets to fulfill this purpose, of which the
intellect has no knowledge.

GLORIA IN EXCELSIS DEO!

A happy person is a gift to the world. When challenges arise, it is easy to set happiness aside for a while. But happiness is a choice I can make regardless of circumstances or events. Choosing happiness is a matter of shifting context, like changing the lenses of eyeglasses from black to rose.

The ego wants to decide what is good or bad, what should make me happy or sad. But I know the source of happiness is within me, even if it seems to be buried deeply some days.

If my house burns down, I can wail and moan and feel sorry for myself even though everything was insured and I will be adequately reimbursed. Or I can choose to view it as an exciting opportunity to start over, perhaps moving to a new part of the country without having to drag all my stuff with me. The external event is the same, my interpretation of the event is volitional.

Before the illness, I had tremendous reserves of mental energy. I would have been dissatisfied if I could only concentrate on writing four hours per day. As health deteriorated, I was grateful for even a single hour of concentration without brain fatigue. A change in context proved that it is the mind that chooses the standard for happiness and gratitude.

I continually pray for strength to make the best of each day, to be happy regardless of external circumstances.

7. LETTING GO OF ATTRACTIONS AND AVERSIONS

DEAR LORD:

It is another fantastic day on which I intend to be happy and radiate kindness to all living beings, especially myself.

I choose to see the divine in all life forms, and I dedicate myself to serving the highest good and receiving divine guidance regarding how I may best serve this purpose each day.

I let go of all attractions and all aversions, and fully experience the joy of life regardless of external events in the world, including the weather and malfunction of electronic devices!

I also let go of all attraction to health and aversion to illness, as well as any

subconscious programs for the opposite:
attraction to illness and aversion to the full
expression of life energy.

GLORIA IN EXCELSIS DEO!

I have read that letting go of attractions
and aversions is a pathway to nonduality,
the dissolution of the ego.

The ultimate challenge to the ego is the threat of
physical extinction. Intention, intense dedication,
and prayer have been required to let go of the attraction
to health and the aversion to illness. It is an
ongoing process in which the deepest fears buried in
the subconscious mind emerge in waves.

But as each level of the fear of death is released,
the existential angst about which the philosophers
have written lessens, and existence becomes lighter
despite pain or the vicissitudes of life. Progressively, I
spend more time in the peaceful state of acceptance,
secure in the knowledge that death of the physical
body has nothing to do with my eternal soul.

8. SENDING LOVE TO THE CELLS

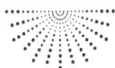

DEAR LORD:

I embrace the knowledge that all is in divine
order at all times regardless of the
opinions of the ego-mind.

I send love to the body's immune system and
thank it for its efforts to protect the body
from what it believes to be foreign
invaders.

I forgive its ignorance in mistaking that which
is self (and must be protected) from that
which is nonself.

I allow the immune system to have perfect
discernment and thank any components of
it that are present in excess for sacrificing
themselves for the good of the whole.

GLORIA IN EXCELSIS DEO!

$\mathcal{I}$n autoimmunity, some of the cells assigned to protect the body from invaders decide that certain cells of the body should be attacked and destroyed. I have read about the incredible, innate intelligence of our cells. What misinformation is causing some of the cells to go rogue? How can it be addressed on the spiritual level?

I have seen videos of the behavior of cells through the lens of a microscope. The cells know what to do without conscious direction from the brain. If the cells innately know what to do, does the intellect need to know if the current experience of autoimmunity involves overactive Th1 cells or Th2 cells? Is it necessary or wise to suppress and destroy them all, which is like punishing the person whose car has been stolen, as well as the thief?

I believe it is beneficial to verbally and mentally appeal directly to the cells of the body's immune system, asking them to resolve their differences. I believe it is helpful to consciously acknowledge their efforts, however misguided, and show appreciation for their vigilance. It cannot interfere with any chosen medical intervention, and it will probably help.

It became a daily practice to talk to the cells, to send them love and to thank the ones that are out of

18

balance for willingly sacrificing themselves to support the good of the whole. I didn't want to express negative intentions towards the rogue cells. I wanted to immerse them in the field of love, so they would choose to serve the good of the whole.

Those who are skeptical about this approach would learn much from the study of quantum physics.

9. LETTING GO OF GUILT

DEAR LORD:

Today, I thank the adrenal glands and the
 entire endocrine system for their perfect
 coordination to maintain circadian
 rhythms that support health and all the
 body's processes.

I accept divine forgiveness for anything that
 resulted in feelings of guilt, either
 conscious or subconscious, that may
 manifest as illness in the body.

I support the body by allowing it to function
 in the parasympathetic mode, fostering
 healing and restoration.

I let go of all guilt, conscious or subconscious,
 that may contribute to misdirecting the
 body to attack itself.

I am thankful for the love and support of
family, friends, neighbors, and perfect
strangers.
GLORIA IN EXCELSIS DEO!

I have read that guilt, conscious or subconscious, is a necessary ingredient for illness to manifest in the body. Eventually, a great source of subconscious guilt bubbled to the surface to be processed.

I had learned at some point in childhood that I was a twin, and that the twin did not fully develop. In stark contrast to the fate of my twin, I survived and came into this world weighing a hefty eight pounds. My mother repeatedly told me my nickname, bestowed by the nurses who dealt with my ravenous appetite in the hospital nursery, was the Baby Elephant.

The innocent mind of the child connected these two events, which were buried in the subconscious mind for decades. The subconscious mind believed that I, the Baby Elephant, literally ate my twin out of house and home. I took all the nourishment, and none was left for her.

When this subconscious belief emerged almost

six decades later, it unleashed a torrent of grief that took days to process and let go. It also sparked the realization that the immune system attacking the body, robbing it of life energy and vitality, could be a subconsciously-initiated form of atonement for taking my twin's life.

It seems that subconscious guilt was one of many conditions that facilitated autoimmune disease, and letting go of the subconscious guilt could help the cells of the immune system heed the positive affirmations I send them through the conscious mind.

10. EXPECTING A MIRACLE, ACCEPTING OUTCOME

DEAR LORD:

I am grateful to see another day and to enjoy the loving support of friends and family.

I am grateful to all the healers who have written books to share their intentions and knowledge directly with the world. I pray for discernment to know which of these paths to pursue from moment to moment to serve the highest good, and I acknowledge that the highest good may not include survival of this physical body.

I am thankful for the body's immune system and admire its innate intelligence and discernment to identify friend and foe with 100% accuracy and to respond appropriately at all times.

I thank the gut for functioning properly and accept the healing energy of the field to optimize the structure and function of the entire digestive system including the liver, kidneys, gallbladder, and microbiome, as well as the esophagus, stomach, and large and small intestines.

I also gratefully accept the miracle of healing in the brain, so all neurotransmitters, hormones, and physiological structures including neurons, axons, dendrites, and synapses operate in perfect harmony with appropriate circadian rhythms.

In particular today, I focus healing attention on the dopamine pathways, the hypothalamus-pituitary-thyroid and hypothalamus-pituitary-adrenal axes, and the neurons that support hearing.

I have 'heard' the message of my current mission in life and respectfully ask the hearing neurons to moderate their firing potential to eliminate tinnitus.

I am thankful to God for unconditional love and opportunities to help alleviate suffering in this world.

I ask the Holy Spirit for support to allow the

physiology of the body to express kindness
to all living beings, including myself.
GLORIA IN EXCELSIS DEO!

I have heard a miracle defined as any event that is beyond the current understanding of science and logic. With that definition, it is not egotistical to expect a miracle. It is opening the mind and heart to healing that the medical community doesn't believe possible.

Early on, I recognized a reticence to ask God for a miracle. Was I afraid that if I wasn't granted a miracle, it meant my belief wasn't strong enough? Was there residual guilt lurking in the subconscious mind that whispered I didn't deserve a miracle?

But my very existence is a miracle that the intellect of man, no matter how developed, does not begin to comprehend. For me, the true miracle of healing was a deep knowingness that it is okay if the body survives and okay if it doesn't. Meanwhile, while it exists, it is my obligation to care for the body to the best of my ability through the application of physical science and the miracle of spirituality.

11. PRAYING FOR OTHERS

Dear Lord:

Thank you for granting me another day on
this beautiful earth.

Please help me see the beauty in every person
and every thing regardless of the opinion
of the ego-mind.

I pray for guidance for all government leaders
at all levels.

I pray for the relief of suffering of all sentient
beings, especially those who are sick,
injured, in pain, lonely, or afraid.

I also pray for strength for those who are
making difficult decisions, that they may
choose the highest good, which I
acknowledge I have no knowledge of.

I thank all the cells of the body and the

microbiome for supporting the highest
health of the body and for any that are
detrimental for graciously sacrificing
themselves to support health of the body.
I freely surrender the life of the body if that
serves the highest good.
Gloria in Excelsis Deo!

It has been helpful to pray for others, as well as for myself, and to ask for help in seeing the divine in everyone. Writing the acknowledgment that the intellect has no way of knowing what serves the highest good helps me recontextualize life challenges and to be accepting of whatever is witnessed from moment to moment.

12. TIPTOEING THROUGH THE EGO

DEAR LORD:

I am so blessed to see another day here and to have an opportunity to serve the highest good.

I pray for guidance from moment to moment each day to discern how to best serve the highest good.

I cancel all detrimental belief systems, conscious or subconscious, including all the detrimental belief systems in the collective consciousness of this world.

I am an infinite being, entitled to enjoy all life's experiences to the fullest extent.

I pray for the strength to write or express information that helps alleviate the suffering of others at a level they can understand.

I pray that I remain exempt from the effects of reprogramming my consciousness with negative belief systems that contribute to illness.

I accept the strength of the Holy Spirit at all times, so the physicality is strong and vigorous enough to serve my highest purpose in life.

At the same time, I release all attachment to outcomes and realize I am an instrument of divine expression on this earth.

I accept whatever health outcome serves the highest good, of which I have no knowledge.

I also release all aversions to full participation in life as well as all attractions to withholding the gifts over which I've been given stewardship in this lifetime: physical, mental, emotional, intellectual, and spiritual.

It is my intention to be unconditionally kind to all of life in all its expressions (including myself) without exception, and to forgive myself when it doesn't happen!

GLORIA IN EXCELSIS DEO!

With practice, the mind has been gradually reprogrammed to recognize the antics of the ego. Eventually, it became possible to explore the uncomfortable topic that there may be some aversion to full health and some attraction to being incapacitated by illness. The willingness to consider this has been big progress, shaking the foundations of the ego.

13. BEING IN THE WORLD, NOT OF IT

DEAR LORD:

It is so easy to get up each morning and get caught up in the day, to produce an adrenaline rush and skip the reflective practice and a calm, relaxing start to the day.

It is my intention to remember at all times that there is no doer, that I am an instrument through which the highest good may be served.

There is no need to rush. All is in divine order.

I pray for the ability to respond appropriately to discernment of my mission in life, and to support the health and vitality of the body so it can serve its spiritual purpose.

I fully embrace the joy of everything life
offers, and enthusiastically use my gifts to
support my mission in life.
I pray for the discernment to guide me in this
intention from moment to moment.
I ask for strength to be in the world but not
of it.
GLORIA IN EXCELSIS DEO!

*A*s the body gained strength it was easy to slip back into old patterns. In the state of extreme challenge it was much easier to intensify spiritual practice and to not be of the world. It was an enforced time-out.

The true test came when the crisis began to subside and enough energy flowed to return to activities in some capacity. But the recognition remained that old patterns no longer served the body or the spirit. It was time to rejoin the world, carrying a deeper spiritual maturity with me.

14. LETTING GO OF PERFECTIONISM

DEAR LORD:

I am grateful to have another day to experience the joy of life and to develop compassion and a nonjudgmental attitude towards all things that seem negative to the ego-mind, which knows nothing.

I ask for guidance to develop discernment to live in the world but not of it, to serve as an instrument for the highest good, and to exist continuously in the full knowledge that there is no doer.

I am thankful for the infinite energy of the field that flows through me and enables the body to carry out its purpose.

I am thankful for the body and remove all blocks to its perfect health and function.

It is my intention to radiate unconditional
love at all times and to be kind to all
beings without exception, including
myself.

I release all guilt associated with being unable
at this level of consciousness to always
fulfill this intention. I accept my
imperfection as a characteristic of being
human.

Please help me release all attractions and
aversions that block my full participation
in, and enjoyment of, this precious gift
of life.

I intellectually understand that all guilt is of
the ego, and I ask the Holy Spirit to
facilitate my release of all guilt, conscious
or subconscious, as well as all negative or
limiting belief systems.

I pray for the strength to fulfill my life mission
without empowering or reenergizing any
negative belief systems or stressful life
patterns.

I affirm that there is no doer and that all is in
divine order at all times.

I am so thankful for the love and support of
other human beings and recognize that full

engagement with others is part of the
journey on this earth.

I accept all loving relationships that further
my development, and I intend to use other
relationships and interactions as a
springboard for spiritual growth rather
than an opportunity for the ego to judge
others.

GLORIA IN EXCELSIS DEO!

Imperfection is part of being human. So is
guilt that we fall short of the goal. After
using physical downtime for spiritual purposes and
feeling that real progress was made, it was a jolt to be
back in the world. Old patterns didn't work anymore,
and new patterns weren't yet firmly established. The
survival of the body was now likely, but full health
was not yet restored. This fragile state brought more
challenges to surrender.

Engaging in what used to be considered a low level of
activity in the world resulted in backsliding of physical
health. And the spiritual state that was acquired in the
solitude of my living room sometimes evaporated when
the clerk at the post office was rude and incompetent!

It was easy to fall into self-judgment and guilt: *I should be healthier, I should have more energy, I should have more patience with the obstacles of daily life.* These are opportunities for me to let go of the *should haves, could haves,* and *would haves*, to live in the moment instead of the past.

All judgment of my progress, both physical and spiritual, is a form of perfectionism. I have heard the spiritual teaching that perfectionism is resistance, a trait of the ego. It always comes back to the ego!

15. BEING GRATEFUL FOR NATURE

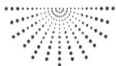

DEAR LORD:

I am grateful to enjoy another miraculous day
here, and I pray for guidance to serve the
highest good from moment to moment all
day long.

I choose to be happy today, to experience
inner joy regardless of external
circumstances of illness or trial, and to be
in the world but not of it.

I am thankful for the exquisite beauty of
nature, for the plants, birds, mountains,
and sky.

I deeply appreciate all the material comforts
of my existence, but I am most grateful for
the love and kindness of family, friends,
and complete strangers.

I hold in mind in the light all those who are
suffering, those who are lonely, those who
are afraid, those who are in pain, those
who are ill, those who are hopeless, and
those who are contemplating suicide.

I release all negative programming, either in
the conscious or subconscious mind.

I release and let go of all blocks to full
participation in this life and pray for
guidance to be the steward of all the gifts I
have been entrusted with.

All is in divine order at all times.

My opinions mean nothing and are of the
ego-mind.

GLORIA IN EXCELSIS DEO!

*T*aking time to absorb the beauty in nature helps restore my soul. It floods the physical body with endorphins and calms the nervous system. And the healing thoughts I send out to the world envelop me, too, because we are all connected.

16. LETTING GO OF RESISTING

DEAR LORD:

I am grateful to be alive.

I thank the immune system for regaining perfect balance and discernment of what is self and what is nonself, what needs to be protected and what does not.

I am thankful for the love and support of family and friends, for the physical sustenance of abundant food, for adequate shelter, for reliable transportation, and for all the conveniences of modern life.

The body absorbs only beneficial energy frequencies. Detrimental energies or sensations pass through the body without effect and are transformed into golden light.

I pray for guidance from moment to moment
to serve the highest good and for the
courage to accept completely all that is
loving and good in life.
I let go resisting all experiences, and I let go
my opinions of good and bad, positive and
negative.

GLORIA IN EXCELSIS DEO!

*L*etting go resisting has helped neutralize, rather than suppress, the ego's negative opinions, facilitating living effortlessly in the flow of life. Autoimmune disease provided plenty of things on which to practice letting go of resistance. There was resistance to sensations of pain and discomfort in the body, drastic changes in lifestyle, the efforts of others to control and direct my journey, and the ignorance of conventional medicine.

And then there was resistance to relapses after progress was made. The ego became attached to the improved health and wanted to judge and figure things out when there was a setback. There has even been resistance to my resistance!

I realize the core of the ego's resistance about illness is fear of suffering and death, both of which pertain to the physical body. There is comfort in reminding myself that I have a body, but I am not a body, and that the body is a temporary vehicle for the eternal soul. When I let go resisting, I am fully alive in the moment, where regrets about the past and fears of the future do not exist.

17. SHIFTING FROM PERCEPTION TO REALITY

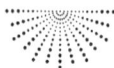

DEAR LORD:

I'm thankful for another glorious day.

It is an opportunity for me to choose to see
the good in everything, to let go resisting
experiences the ego deems negative, and to
honor the body that is the vehicle for my
divine soul.

I'm grateful for all the blessings in my life, and
I ask the Holy Spirit for discernment to
serve the highest good this day and
every day.

I cancel all negative belief systems, both
conscious and subconscious.

I am an infinite being, exempt from all
negative beliefs.

Today I rest in the healing energy of the field

of infinite love and kindness and intend to transmit these positive energies in thought, word, and deed.

GLORIA IN EXCELSIS DEO!

The lenses through which I perceive life define what I believe is real. As I progress spiritually, I realize that perception and reality are not the same thing.

The favorite prey of the Bengal tiger is a deer that has dichromatic vision, so the deer perceives the tiger as shadowy gray stripes that blend with the rippling foliage of the jungle. Humans who aren't colorblind have trichromatic vision and perceive the tiger as orange. Which perception is reality?

Examining, challenging, and dismantling belief systems progressively shifts my perception of reality and helps dissolve the ego. It is a continuous process.

18. REALIZING ALL IS IN DIVINE ORDER

DEAR LORD:

I'm thankful for the gift of another glorious day on this earth.

I pray for the certain knowledge that all is in divine order at all times, even when the ego-mind wants to label everything as good or bad.

I release all fear, especially the fear of physical pain.

I ask for discernment, so I can take appropriate action without attachment to outcome, rather than falling into apathy and nonaction.

I accept all actions of others towards me, either pleasant or unpleasant, as spiritual lessons.

I pray for the relief of suffering of all sentient
  beings, including myself.
I asked the Holy Spirit to help me let go of all
  resistance, all desire to control outcomes
  for myself and others, and all opinions.
I also ask for guidance this day on how to
  serve the highest good from moment to
  moment.
GLORIA IN EXCELSIS DEO!

The most useful and comforting spiritual phrase for me is *all is in divine order*. And because it is so difficult for the ego to accept this simple truth, I repeat it often throughout the day. It appears in many of these letters to God.

I remind myself that because God created this world, it is perfect. It is only the human ego that wants to know why and assign blame. The mind of God cannot be expressed through, or comprehended by, the human intellect. It requires an open and nonjudgmental heart.

19. SUFFERING IS OPTIONAL

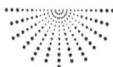

DEAR LORD:

I feel confident, calm and peaceful as I realize each moment is in divine perfection, even if the human intellect wants to judge and say otherwise.

I realize that physical pain does not need to equate to suffering. That is a choice of the ego-mind.

As I release all judgment, I feel all the molecules in the body aligning in perfect coherence to support physical healing and restoration.

The adrenal glands have boundless energy and resources to support all healing functions of the body, because they have been

released from constant vigilance to
respond in fight-or-flight mode.

The heart, brain, and gut operate in perfect
harmony now that the mind, both
conscious and subconscious, stops trying
to control events and circumstances.

I ask for the gift of discernment to live each
moment of this day serving the highest
good to the best of my abilities at
this time.

I am grateful for the love and support of
others and feel compassion for those who
project their negativity towards me or
others in the world.

I pray for the relief of suffering of all sentient
beings, including myself.

Gloria in Excelsis Deo!

I have heard that pain and suffering are not
conjoined twins, they can be separated!
Pain is a neutral sensation recorded by the mind.
The optional association of fear and negative
emotions with the sensations I call pain result in
suffering. Although the concept of separating the

sensation of physical pain from suffering is simple, the actual practice of releasing the negative emotions attached to pain has required practice. It has been helpful to let go resisting the physical sensations by witnessing them without applying the label of *pain*.

20. DIVINE IDIOCY?

Dear Lord:

Thank you for the gift of another day on
this earth.

I let go of all opinions of the intellect, which
cannot comprehend the mind of God.

I move through the day immersed in your
divine light, secure in the knowledge that
all is in divine order at all times, no matter
what the ego-mind wants to think.

I choose joy today. I release all attractions to
all programs and belief systems, conscious
or subconscious, that are a barrier to
continuous joyfulness regardless of
circumstances.

I ask the Holy Spirit for strength to release
judgment of myself and others.

I am thankful for the love and support of
family, friends, and strangers.
Today I live in constant awareness that there
is no doer and that my intentions and total
acceptance of divine will without
resistance, opinion, or judgment will allow
the highest good to manifest through me
as your instrument on this earth.
GLORIA IN EXCELSIS DEO!

*T*he intellect is powerful and has been a useful tool in life. I have been very attached to the intellect.

Autoimmunity caused brain inflammation and impaired the ability to participate in life as it was once experienced. Information processing, regulation of body processes, physical stamina, and coordination were all affected. It was an opportunity to examine the belief systems about the true nature of existence and the soul, to discern what actions should be taken to repair the damage, and to deeply realize that I am not the intellect.

I have heard serious spiritual students say that one must lose the intellect on the road to enlightenment, and I have heard this state called divine idiocy, in which normal brain function is impossible. When it was suggested that my impaired brain function should be welcomed as a state of divine idiocy, the discernment was that mine was a case of simple idiocy! If it had been divine idiocy, there wouldn't have been enough ego left to think about it.

Mistaking brain damage from illness for an exalted spiritual state would have precluded action, an error in judgment at my current level of consciousness.

21. MICROSOFT AS SPIRITUAL TEACHER!

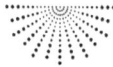

DEAR LORD:

Thank you for another beautiful day on this planet.

Thank you for the lessons yesterday in releasing willfulness regarding schedules and accomplishments.

I ask for improved discernment to see the spiritual lessons in all things and all events, every day and every moment.

I thank you for Microsoft and my computer as delivery instruments for spiritual lessons! You sure have a sense of humor!

Please help me be continuously aware that there is no doer, that I am an instrument to employ my gifts through my free will to serve the highest good.

Please help me continuously be aware that my
opinions mean absolutely nothing.
I pray for the relief of suffering of all sentient
beings on the planet.
GLORIA IN EXCELSIS DEO!

*D*ealing month after month with the continuous stream of debilitating symptoms of autoimmunity brought up anger to be processed. The ego was definitely not happy with the turn of events and the fact that there were no quick fixes. The ego was willful and wanted to control the situation.

There was enough spiritual development to prefer not to vent anger inappropriately (although that certainly happened at times). The clever ego found a socially-acceptable target for anger: Windows 10! A quick Google search of problems encountered with Windows 10 verified I wasn't the only one frustrated by forced updates that cause random computer problems and interfere with productivity.

Microsoft and Windows 10 became my spiritual teachers. We met weekly on what I called Woeful Wednesdays, the aftereffect of Terrible Tuesdays, when involuntary system updates to Windows 10 are delivered. The random havoc many of these updates wreaked on my two Windows computers sometimes took hours to unravel.

I unleashed explosions of criticism of the software and its originator. *What kind of company would inflict this torture on its customers? Didn't anybody review this stuff before they released it? How dare they hijack my computer against my will? Take this subscription and place it somewhere that will make it very uncomfortable to sit!*

Each week, Windows 10 gave me an opportunity to rant and rave, puff up the ego, and have a fabulous judgment extravaganza!

And then the realization dawned that I could stop resisting the whole process. This immediately shifted the context: I could write courses for my continuing education business on how to manage Windows 10.

The sudden shift of context from negative to positive, the realization that I could make the best of a situation I couldn't change and make money in the process, only came when I stopped resisting Windows 10!

22. LETTING GO OF THE JUDGE

DEAR LORD:

Thank you for granting me another glorious day on this earth.

Thank you for granting me the discernment to be the best steward of my gifts in the service of the highest good.

I pray for the relief of suffering of all sentient beings on the planet, including myself.

Please help me release all attractions and aversions, to participate fully in life, and to express express compassion and kindness for all.

I pray to always be secure in the knowledge that all is in divine order at all times.

GLORIA IN EXCELSIS DEO!

*P*racticing compassion and kindness towards others distracts the mind from the internal situation and helps me let go resisting what is happening in the body.

But there are times when it is difficult for me to practice compassion. When conventional medicine was ignorant of the full-body effects of autoimmunity, it brought out the judge in me, and compassion flew out the window. Just as the spiritual ego thought it was earning its halo, it became obvious there was a long way to go!

I have heard the spiritual teaching that judgment is never justified, that all error is due to ignorance. Sometimes it is difficult to let go of the judge, so it helps to go back to the teaching that my opinions mean nothing.

I realize that the seat of all annoyance is within me. It is independent of external events, which offer a seemingly justifiable outlet for judgment. When I get frustrated with someone, I need to look in the mirror and let go of something in myself. I guess that's why it's called spiritual *practice*. Practice, practice, practice!

23. STEWARDING GIFTS

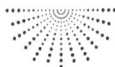

DEAR LORD:

I am again grateful for another day, and I align
    my intentions to serve the highest good.

I intend to see the divine in others at all
    times, without exception, as well as in
    myself.

I rest in the knowingness that there is no
    doer, that all is in divine order at all times,
    that all opinions and thoughts are
    projections of the ego and are therefore
    meaningless.

I let go of all attractions and aversions while
    participating fully and joyfully in life, free
    from conscious or subconscious guilt
    about the gifts I have been granted.

I ask for guidance on how to be the best

steward of these gifts to serve the highest
good.
It is my intention to honor myself in body,
mind, and spirit, regardless of the
judgment or opinions of others.

GLORIA IN EXCELSIS DEO!

We are all born with gifts. Mine included a keen intellect and an incredible abundance of energy. Autoimmunity delivered numerous opportunities to lessen the attachment to these gifts, to realize that intellect and energy are of the body and are temporary, and to realize that I have a body, but I am not a body.

Illness has also offered the opportunity to release guilt that I had such abundance while many others did not, as well as guilt that I am attached to my gifts and include them in the identification of what I am.

As a spiritual student, I acknowledge that at an intellectual level all gifts in the material world are on loan from the universe. Illness helped me transform this intellectual knowledge to deeper levels of experiential reality and to lessen the attachment to the material world, including the body.

I have met those who believe that surrendering

the attachments to gifts on the physical plane means they must be negated. However, I have heard that only the *attachment* to one's gifts is to be surrendered, not the gifts themselves.

My own experience has been that each level of surrender to attachments in the physical plane has brought me greater enjoyment of my gifts. Knowing and accepting that the body will age and ultimately retire itself allows me to enjoy it today and waste less energy worrying about the future. And letting go of the attachment to material things removes the fear of their loss, which is ultimately inevitable.

24. EXPRESSING GRATITUDE FOR SLEEP

DEAR LORD:

I am thankful for a night of delicious, deep, restful sleep.

I am thankful for the perfect circadian rhythms in the body that enable me to enjoy a lovely night of uninterrupted sleep that rejuvenates body, mind, and soul.

I intend to serve the highest good today to the best of my abilities, and I pray for discernment to know what form this service takes from moment to moment.

I release all fear, anxiety, and judgment, and I intend to envelop myself and others in loving kindness, without exception.

I resolve to be the instrument through which my unique gifts manifest this day to

support the highest good, and I let go of
all opinions the ego-mind formulates,
secure in the knowingness that all is in
divine order at all times.
GLORIA IN EXCELSIS DEO!

*H*umans require sleep. Americans often
brag about how little they need to sleep
as they keep to their busy schedules. They view sleep
deprivation as a badge of courage or accept it as a
condition of modern life.

I have never felt the urge to participate in the
cultural contest of sleep deprivation. It was devas-
tating when autoimmunity trashed the body's circadian rhythms through imbalances in
neurotransmitters, cortisol levels, and blood sugar. In
turn, lack of sleep impaired function of brain and
body, and it affected mood and personality. It was a
downward spiral.

For almost a year sleep became elusive and
random. Sleep problems persisted despite dietary
changes, meditation, relaxation techniques, and self-
hypnosis. I had to surrender to the lack of sleep, to
practice living in the moment without judgment even
in the middle of the night when I preferred oblivion

to experiencing!

I came to the realization that lying in bed feeling stressed about how lack of sleep would affect the coming day was not conducive to healing. Once I realized that how I viewed lack of sleep was a choice, I decided to make the best of the situation.

Many nights, I opened the shutters and spent hours gazing up at the moon or the Milky Way through the bedroom window, marveling at the vastness of the universe and the stillness of the night. It was a time for meditation and contemplation, and it offered the chance to express gratitude that I didn't have to go to an office and work the next day. It allowed me to feel compassion for others suffering the same way who had daily responsibilities and a regular job.

25. EMBRACING THE LESSONS OF CRISIS

DEAR LORD:

I am thankful for another day of precious life.

I choose to be happy today, no matter how I
feel or what happens.

I intend to be productive today in alignment
with the highest good.

I pray for the discernment to understand what
form that takes.

I am secure in the knowledge that all is in
divine order at all times.

I pray for assistance to let go resisting crisis,
to live each moment fully and without
question or opinion, and to radiate love
and kindness for myself and others.

GLORIA IN EXCELSIS DEO!

I have heard, and practiced to the best of my ability, the spiritual teaching to live fully in the moment. I had made progress, and the ego had lessened its grip on questioning the past and projecting into the future.

But when survival of the body, with which the ego identifies, was threatened, I had numerous opportunities to practice living in the moment at a deeper level. It seemed like I had unwittingly enrolled in an accelerated course without taking the necessary prerequisites. *Did I ask for this? Did I manifest this illness?* Not specifically, but I did declare a spiritual commitment to God with the intention to use this life for spiritual advancement.

Who am I to question or judge the circumstances that unfold to best support my spiritual intention? The crisis of illness has been a crash course in spirituality. That might be bad from the perspective of the ego, but it is real progress for the Self.

26. SURRENDERING IMPATIENCE

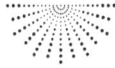

DEAR LORD:

Thank you for another day on this earth.

I pray for guidance and discernment in all
areas today.

I intend to support the body's health, to foster
parasympathetic dominance, to provide all
nutrients, thoughts, beliefs systems,
emotions, and conditions that support
healing and perfect health.

I release aversions to illness, and I accept
whatever degree of health results.

I rest in the comfort that all is in divine order
at all times and that my thoughts and
opinions mean nothing.

Please help me to be mindful of the fact that
speed and impatience are of the ego, as

expressed through the chemistry of the
brain and body.

It is my intention to surrender the willfulness
that lies behind impatience, therefore
shifting the physiology of brain and body
to a state of peace, happiness, and
surrender.

I intend to use each experience this day as an
opportunity for spiritual growth and to
stay in the witness with benevolence
towards myself and others, no matter
what.

GLORIA IN EXCELSIS DEO!

A Course in Miracles teaches that I have a body,
I am not a body. The body I have was pre-wired for fight or flight, expressed in the body as
dominance of the sympathetic nervous system. It
began in utero when my mother's body, and therefore
the developing embryo that became me, was flooded
with stress hormones when she discovered during the
first trimester of pregnancy that her father had brain
cancer.

Until recently, the natural state of the body was
governed by an excess of neurotransmitters that

scream *go, go, go* and a deficiency of neurotransmitters that whisper *slow, slow, slow*. The result was impatience, lots and lots of impatience.

It has been a gift to understand that impatience is part of the biochemical individuality of the body, that it not of the Self, that it can be surrendered, and that neuronal pathways in the brain can be rewired for peace.

27. LETTING GO OF THE DOER

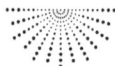

Dear Lord:

I am thankful and grateful for the insights
revealed to me every morning as I awaken.
They reinforce that there is no doer, that
my thoughts and opinions are of the ego
and mean nothing, and that intention and
surrender will allow my mission on this
earth to be fulfilled through me, not
by me.

I realize that all is in divine order at all times,
that it is counterproductive to waste
energy and stress the body through fear or
resistance of any sort.

At all times, I will be taken care of in a way
that suits the circumstances.

I let go of all guilt, apprehension, fear,

opinions, and willfulness, and relax into
the field confident that all that unfolds
serves the highest good no matter what
it is.

I surrender the opinions of how, when, and
even if, what I perceive to be my life's
mission is accomplished.

It is my intention to be in the world, not of it;
to always realize the precious gift that is
given with each day on earth; and to be
patient, kind, and gentle with myself and
with others.

I ask for the continuing support of the Holy
Spirit so I may exist as joy and peace
regardless of the turbulence of external
events or the state of the physical body.

GLORIA IN EXCELSIS DEO!

I have heard the spiritual teaching that there is no doer, that all emerges spontaneously when conditions are appropriate, and one of those conditions is intention.

Even when I was in the business world I realized there are forces that are not of the self, that are not volitional, that are activated by intention. During the day I would process information with the intellect, intending to solve the problem I was hired to evaluate. The best realizations came when the intellect was turned off: during dreams delivered in sleep, as images downloaded during the hypnagogic state between sleep and wakefulness, as bolts from the blue when I was pulling weeds in the garden.

Serious illness reinforced that there is no doer, but it also reinforced it was appropriate for me to use the intellect to till the soil to prepare it to receive the seeds of discernment, which could be allowed to grow into the blossoms of action without attachment to outcome.

28. BEING GRATEFUL FOR ALL THAT IS

DEAR LORD:

I am grateful for the wonderful sleep I had
last night.

I am grateful for my cozy, comfortable home,
which has been a lovely cocoon that
shelters me in the long process of healing
the body and experiencing the evolution of
consciousness.

I am grateful for the love and support of
friends and family.

I am grateful for all the people who wrote
books and published information that
make physical healing of the body possible.

I am grateful for Dr. David Hawkins and all
the spiritual teachers whose work helps me
contextualize this life on earth and

recognize the spiritual opportunity of
illness and adversity.

I am grateful for the guidance of the Holy
Spirit, for the gift of discernment, and for
my life's mission: to ease human suffering
by integrating the physiological and the
spiritual.

GLORIA IN EXCELSIS DEO!

I have made it a point to cultivate an attitude of gratitude. I know that things can always be more difficult than they are right now. Expressing gratitude helps me release the juice of self-pity and victimhood, and it opens the door to spiritual progress.

29. RELEASING ATTACHMENT TO OUTCOME

DEAR LORD:

Please help me understand that there is no doer, but that at the same time, I exercise my free will and set intentions.

I am responsible for effort but not outcome.

I release all attachment to outcome as I enthusiastically embrace action to fulfill my life's mission.

I remind myself that all is in divine order.

I hold in mind with compassion all who are suffering from loss of a loved one, illness, anxiety, or fear.

I have compassion for myself and release self-judgment.

May we all rest secure in God's infinite love.

GLORIA IN EXCELSIS DEO!

I have repeatedly heard the spiritual teaching that we are responsible for the effort but not the outcome, that attachment to outcome is of the ego. It was startling to realize that praying for a specific outcome for myself or others (recovery from illness, passing a test, catching a bus, etc.) meant that the ego thinks it is smarter than God!

At first, the ego resisted this idea, but upon frank examination, it resonated as truth. It was humorous to imagine an anthropomorphic God sitting on a cloud, fielding millions of messages per second beaming up from planet Earth: *Don't let me burn dinner when my in-laws are visiting; Help me get this house; Let me have this job and I will go to church every Sunday for a year; Please make this dye turn my hair the perfect shade of blonde!*

I have heard it is appropriate to pray for spiritual strength and the relief of suffering of all sentient beings, rather than trying to direct outcome, which is telling God what to do. It has helped to go back to the basic teaching that my opinions mean nothing. I don't know if it serves the highest good for me to completely recover, to hang around another couple of decades with ill health, or to check out today.

It is a huge relief when I realize I don't have to know! I can take all the energy I used to spend directing God on how to run the world and just accept how it is. I am only responsible for the effort, and I can surrender the outcome to God.

30. THROUGH ME, NOT BY ME

DEAR LORD:

This day I am grateful for the improved health
of the physical body and the deep spiritual
lessons that can be learned from crisis.

As I improve in vigor and stamina, I intend to
continue to live the lessons: to live without
criticizing the past or being anxious about
the future; to appreciate all is in divine
order at all times regardless of what the
ego thinks; to be kind and compassionate
to myself and others to the extent I
am able.

As always, I am grateful for the many gifts I
have: love, friendship, inner tranquility.

When peace and tranquility are temporarily
disturbed due to physiological imbalances

in neurotransmitters, I ask for strength to
let that go without judgment and to
develop compassion for others who are
doing the best they can with the resources
at their disposal.

I ask for help to live my life always
recognizing that there is no doer, that my
intention to let go of willfulness and
opinion allows the highest good to be
served through me, not by me.

I pray for the relief of suffering (physical,
mental, emotional, and spiritual) of all
sentient beings, including myself.

GLORIA IN EXCELSIS DEO!

The *willfulness* of ego *thinks* things are
accomplished *by* me. The *willingness* of
Spirit *knows* things are accomplished *through* me. It
always comes back to letting go of the ego.

In my case, the ego frequently appears in the
guise of willfulness, of attachment to outcome. Every
day brings dozens of opportunities to recognize willfulness and shift into willingness. Every day, I ask for
divine assistance to let go of all blocks to willingness.

31. PRAYING FOR DISCERNMENT

DEAR LORD:

I am thankful for another day of life on
this earth.

I am grateful that there is less pain in the body
today than there was yesterday.

I am grateful for the lesson that I need to
surrender willfulness and shift into
intention and willingness to use my gifts to
serve the highest good without opinion or
attachment to outcome.

I am thankful for the teaching that all is in
divine order at all times, regardless of the
chatter of the ego-mind, which wants
to judge.

I am thankful for all the people who have
written books with the intention to relieve

human suffering, and I'm grateful to learn this information. I pray for discernment to know which of these conflicting recommendations (if any) are best for me at this time.

GLORIA IN EXCELSIS DEO!

There are so many conflicting recommendations about how to manage autoimmune disease. It seemed overwhelming, especially when the brain was inflamed and operating at reduced capacity.

As I expressed gratitude for all the doctors and other health professionals who wrote books to share their knowledge directly with the public, I prayed for discernment to know which recommendations were best for me. Gratitude and intention facilitated the delivery of valuable information that presented itself in the right form at the right time.

The intellect processed the information, but it was a nonlinear inner knowingness that indicated what was best for me at the time. The process has been a lesson in acknowledging the value of science and the intellect without negation of the value of intention and intuition.

32. PATIENCE, PLEASE!

DEAR LORD:

I am grateful for the love and support of
family and friends and the kindness of
strangers, all of which enrich my life and
lighten the challenges we all encounter.

I pray for the gifts of patience and kindness
for myself and others.

GLORIA IN EXCELSIS DEO!

I have heard the spiritual teaching that
impatience is of the ego, that it is resistance to what is happening in the moment and
wanting circumstances to be other than what they
are. It became obvious that impatience was just will-

fulness in disguise, and letting go of willfulness is my major life lesson.

Autoimmunity has been a continuous opportunity to surrender impatience. There has been impatience with lack of healing progress, impatience with others who don't understand what I am dealing with, impatience with overwhelming and often conflicting advice on the Internet, and impatience with fluctuating energy levels that sometimes make it impossible to commit to activities most other people don't even need to think about.

When a hyperthyroid state was experienced, revving body and brain to warp speed, it was a humbling realization that impatience is partly biochemical, that it is impersonal and not a part of the Self. It helped me view impatience in myself and others without judgment and to pray for the gift of patience.

33. ALIGNING WITH PURPOSE

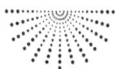

DEAR LORD:

I am thankful for another glorious day on this
earth, and I pray for discernment to align
with my divine purpose.

I'm thankful for insights on how to be the
best steward of my assets in this life,
including the intellect and my accumulated
life experiences.

It is my intention to allow inspiration to flow
through me without interference from the
ego-mind.

I pray for forgiveness from God, from any I
may have harmed, and from myself.

I realize that guilt is a form of egoism, that
regret for transgressions and intention to
do better is all that is required of me.

I pray for the release of guilt in all its forms,
   conscious or subconscious, that I may
   better serve the highest good.
I also pray for the continuous confidence that
   all is in divine order at all times, regardless
   of the mind's opinion of good or bad.
I intend to live this day ever mindful that my
   opinion means nothing and to be open to
   divine inspiration and guidance.
GLORIA IN EXCELSIS DEO!

*S*cientific studies show that serving a purpose in life is beneficial to mental and physical health. Even the purpose of caring for a pet improves longevity. Work, helping others, gardening, cooking, and spiritual practice were enjoyable and provided purpose in life before illness struck.

However, at its nadir, the function of the body barely supported life. Everything was experienced through the haze of brain inflammation, and every bone and joint in the body ached. Heart rate rose to its maximum safe level just walking from the sofa to the kitchen. For months, the physical activities that once provided purpose in life became impossible.

It was easy for the ego to hit the panic button, to

say that the situation was dire, to judge it as bad and resist the experience of it. But the slowed brain function and lack of endurance increased alignment with spiritual practice. The physical body was grounded on the sofa, and the grip on the linear was lessened.

Continual surrender and openness to divine inspiration regarding my purpose in life and my willingness to follow divine guidance facilitated the spontaneous appearance of vital information that helped the body eventually recover to a much greater extent than would be expected.

I am grateful for all physical healing, and I pray for guidance on how I can best use the improved physical capacity to serve the highest good.

34. WITNESSING BEAUTY

Dear Lord:

I am thankful for the opportunity to witness the beautiful sunrise illuminating the mists across the valley, for the soothing sounds of birds calling, and for the peace and serenity of this home I am privileged to live in.

I ask for guidance this day how to best use my gifts to serve the highest good.

I pray for discernment and the constant awareness that there is no doer, that all is in divine order at all times, and that the way is clear when the chatter of the mind is surrendered.

I pray for the strength to be in the world, but

not of it, and to always replace willfulness with willingness to serve.

GLORIA IN EXCELSIS DEO!

I have heard that beauty is a pathway to God. I appreciate esthetics, and it is especially easy for me to access beauty through the colors, textures, and forms in nature. A daily beauty bath has been healing to the inflamed brain, gently exercising the neuronal pathways responsible for vision, hearing, touch, and smell.

I have chosen to use the forced inactivity of illness to spend more time observing beauty and less time being willful about accomplishing daily tasks or reaching work goals.

One of my favorite images of beauty was a rainbow in the valley below my home. I let go of the intention to work that day and instead witnessed the rainbow. It lasted for four hours, shifting and changing shape and location as the day wore on, responding to the angle of the sun as it filtered through the mist. At times, the rainbow was starkly illuminated against the background of dark storm clouds. At other times, patches of blue sky and puffs of white clouds were visible, punctuated by arcs of rainbow.

The return on investment of time I spend witnessing beauty is incalculable. I often choose to re-experience the images of beauty in the mind, triggering beneficial physiological responses that lessen the perception of pain and calm anxieties when they arise. This miraculous narcotic is free, has no adverse side effects, and requires only my willingness to experience it.

35. LETTING GO OF THE TASKMASTER OF TIME

DEAR LORD:

Thank you for the gift of this beautiful day.

Please help me discern what intentions serve the highest good and what actions are appropriate today to fulfill those intentions.

Please help me let go of attachment to outcome, of attachment to timeframes, of attachment to self-judgment about it all.

Please help me let go of the attachment to the very concept of time and the aversion to the perception of insufficient achievement as measured by time.

Please help me let go of impatience with myself, to accept what is today.

Please help me remember that all is in divine

order, to accept what arises in each
moment, and to welcome (not resist) the
flow of events as they emerge.

Please help me surrender to what is, to find
joy in existence regardless of the state of
the physical body, the capacity of the
brain, or accomplishment in the linear
world.

GLORIA IN EXCELSIS DEO!

I once had tireless mental and physical energy, and I took it for granted. Illness brought me to a screeching halt and gave me a literal time-out to contemplate why we are on this planet. The capacity to function was restricted to an hour or so per day.

Now I exist in an unpredictable twilight zone in which functionality is greatly improved but not reliable enough to indulge my old habits of planning ahead, setting deadlines, and meeting goals. The unpredictable see-saw of energy levels is my lesson to find joy in existence exactly as it is in each moment, to let go of attachment to the taskmaster of time, and to release the identification of self with achievements.

I have no idea what the future brings: I may get better, I may get worse, I may die next week. I enjoy the life I have in this moment and live without fear of what the future holds, because I have surrendered the outcome to God. Illness has served its spiritual purpose, and God has answered my letters.

On the surface, Patricia A. Lynch, who earned a BS in Chemical Engineering from the University of Illinois at Urbana-Champaign and an MBA from the University of Chicago, seems an unlikely candidate to author a book on spirituality. Patricia, known to family and friends as Trish, had varied careers in the business world.

In her early forties, the willfulness and determination Trish had mistakenly credited for her business success took a physical toll. Two years in a row, she became very ill after returning to the harsh winter climate in Chicago after business trips to balmy southeast Asia. Jokingly, she observed that if it happened a third year, the Man Upstairs was telling her she should do something else with her life. Right on schedule the following winter, the message was delivered with a bang when she became very ill after another international business trip.

Following her intuition, Trish jumped off the fast-track with no idea of what she would do next. A ten-year sabbatical ensued during which she sought physical healing for herself and was present for friends and family members who were gravely ill. Observing how each person handled death of the physical body rekindled a latent interest in spirituality.

Trish began to study the great spiritual traditions of the world, found the work of Dr. David R. Hawkins, and practiced the techniques Dr. Hawkins describes in his book, *Letting Go: The Pathway to Surrender*. When she became very ill with an autoimmune disease in 2016, she viewed it as an opportunity to transform the crisis into broader spiritual awareness.

Career-wise, she now identifies herself as a writer. But her higher calling and priority is the spiritual path, which is enriched by spending time with family and friends and enjoying the beauty of nature. She lives in Arizona and Illinois, enjoying the contrast between the terrains, climates, and lifestyles unique to each location. Learn more about the author and her upcoming books at www.Patricia-A-Lynch.com.

www.ingramcontent.com/pod-product-compliance
Lightning Source LLC
Chambersburg PA
CBHW021206020426
42331CB00003B/235